Contemplations
on the Self

Contemplations and illustrations by

A. Saranagati

one sOurce press

ISBN: 978-0-578-43806-1

PRINTED IN THE UNITED STATES OF AMERICA

Invocation

In veneration of Ramana Maharshi, whose life, teachings
and eternal presence are the ultimate contemplation.

The single-most desire that all human beings share is to be ever happy and free of suffering. Consequently, our life journey is one of attempting to fulfill this basic requisite. The question then arises — *Is happiness found in the world outside of ourselves or is it innate and ever present within us?*

Self-inquiry is a means of answering this question. It is a simple yet often challenging way of redirecting the outward-turned mind onto its source — the self, which is referred to in various traditions as God, Brahman, Jehovah, Allah, Buddha nature, Christ consciousness and the Light. The way is simple in that the instruction is easy to understand and follow, but challenging in that our tendencies, or habits of the mind, often sabotage our effort. Self-inquiry involves investigating *Who am I?* to quiet the mind while, at the same time, divest the false sense we have of ourselves of its authority. This question is not intended to be a repeated mantra but rather an impetus to begin the inquiry. Redirecting the mind onto itself can be likened to swimming upstream against the current when we are accustomed to simply floating downstream. If the mind is restless or drowsy, the attempt to swim against the current of thoughts is futile. However, when the mind is alert and still, the current is not detectable and swimming upstream is effortless.

As we begin self-inquiry, we become aware of the rapid rate at which our thoughts proliferate, moving from past activities and concerns to the future and back again, barely hesitating while passing over the present moment. We can also single out the central thought from which all other thoughts arise. This thought, which we call "I", is our ego. It comprises the mind, which can be seen as simply a jumble of thoughts, and the body, which the ego arbitrarily identifies itself to be. The ego takes full credit for the cognitive skills of the brain, which are separate and distinct from the mind, while its constant mind chatter provides the means for it to maintain a position of control. As a result, the false sense of being a distinct and separate individual is born.

The ego evaluates everything it encounters and, based on previous encounters, rates each as pleasing, indifferent or displeasing. Observing the ego, we see that its appearances are intermittent, mutable and impermanent, similar to a cloud in the sky. Consequently, it cannot be real though we mistake it as such and give it full rein to govern our lives. We also notice its perceptions are based on duality. In other words, each of its perceptions requires an opposite, a polar complement; for there to be things that please the ego, there must be things of equal measure that displease it.

When observing the thinker, or ego, our habitual tendencies often come to the fore, such as an unexpected awareness of being impatient, judgmental, irritable or selfish. This might discourage us from continuing our inquiry or cause us to become self-critical and then analyze or attempt to alter our tendencies. But using the mind to correct the mind would be like asking the thief disguised as a policeman to catch the thief. So, instead of altering or running away from our tendencies, we continue our pursuit and still the mind by seeking the thinker, or finding from where its thoughts arise, or simply letting the thoughts go.

As the mind winds down, we notice that problems are easier to resolve, creative ideas come more readily and making plans is less complicated. Engaging in any of these endeavors, however, invites the ego's return and terminates our inquiry. By resisting this temptation, we soon discover for ourselves that resolution, creativity and planning take place spontaneously in the complete absence of the ego.

Still another potential deviation from our inquiry occurs when we find ourselves entangled in the endless stories of the ego or its conversations with itself that can last anywhere from a few moments to extended periods of time. While some of the repetitive themes of these stories may seem to be pacifying, they all stimulate the mind creating restlessness or drowsiness. Some stories deceive us with their sense of urgency and importance or with their noble aspirations. We might feel as though we get pulled into them by a compelling force without our even being aware of it. Yet this force is just a conditioned reaction of the mind that distracts us from the sublime yet continuous force that draws us to the self, like the force of gravity that pulls objects to the earth. Confronting the ego straight on takes a great effort that requires undying patience, humility and fortitude. Perhaps it is as great as the effort we made when we were first learning to walk. Then, despite countless failures, we persisted until we achieved our goal. Such determination is needed again to achieve the greater quest of self-realization.

Each time we focus on the thinker, it disappears only to quickly reappear in a different guise. The thinker's erratic appearances can be likened to a gopher peeping its head out of a hole. When a cat lunges toward it, instantly it disappears only to reappear from another of its many holes. If we become disheartened by our initial inability to maintain concentration, we need to inquire, *Who is discouraged?* If the discouraged one is not found to be everlasting, can it be real? Challenging the existence of the ego in this way provides invaluable insights into our essential nature. If we wonder who is making this inquiry, it is the ego looking for itself. When it cannot be found, its elusive existence ceases and the self alone remains. Similar to the stick used as a poker to stir a fire, the ego eventually burns itself up.

The objective of most spiritual traditions and psychological practices is to understand the ego, or disarm it of its dominance, or, at the very least, divest it of its considered "undesirable" aspects. On the other hand, self-inquiry aims to destroy the ego altogether. This is not done with disdain, considering that its illusive existence manifests from the self and, consequently, is not apart from it. The ego has inadvertently been mistaken to be the self. The analogy often used to explain this paradox is that of a coiled rope appearing to be a snake. The rope and the snake are not separate entities. However, without careful investigation, the rope is believed to be the snake in the same way that the ego is believed to be the self. What needs to be destroyed is our false identification with the ego. However, we're not inclined to challenge its position of authority, much less destroy it, for fear of losing it. We assume the ego provides a function that we cannot live without, even though we can clearly observe that its mental chatter only hinders awareness. For the ego to exist, it must grasp onto things external to itself — objects, thoughts, sensations. Turning the attention onto the ego by seeking its origin disables its ability to grasp. Hence, it disappears leaving only the self.

We have been conditioned to believe that consciousness is found in the physical body. Yet the fact remains that distinctions cannot be made between our consciousness and that of others; consciousness is singular and exactly the same in all beings. The consciousness of the ego is only a superficial reflection of the pure, ever-shining consciousness of the self. The analogy often used to clarify this phenomenon is the luminosity of the moon being solely the reflected light of the sun. Besides utilizing the consciousness of the self, the ego takes full advantage of the self's knowledge, which is revealed through the silent language of the intuition, by manipulating this knowledge to conform to the ego's ever-changing perceptions and beliefs.

Our attachment to the ego is said to be the addiction that surpasses all others. The ego identifies itself as the physical body, which is constantly changing and has no lasting existence in and of itself. On the other hand, we are certain of our existence, since it always is and has never changed. It is continuous throughout the sleep, dream and waking states, whereas the body that appears in the waking state disappears altogether in the other states. We are continuous existence. The body is discontinuous and is part of the ever-changing phenomenal world. Ironically, we fear breaking our addiction to the ego even though we do it everyday when we go to sleep. In fact, we long for the deep sleep in which the ego does not exist, though we are fully present, and value that time as the most precious of our greatest pleasures.

Wherever we happen to be throughout the course of our daily lives, we inquire to find the origin of our habitual tendencies and consequent mental states. *Who is irritated right now? Who is judging or feeling pain? Who is thinking?* During this continuous meditation in which we take the position of a silent witness, we develop an ability to simply observe thoughts as they arise in the mind without thinking about them. From this vantage point, we see that there is really no one to whom the mental states belong and the culprit responsible for their appearances is none other than the imagined sense we have of ourselves.

As our habitual tendencies diminish along with the mind chatter, our point of view broadens and our attention moves closer to the present moment where the ego has nowhere to hide. The hard edges of our perceptions soften, which enables us to trust in what lies beyond them. Upon realizing the ego has been the sole obstruction to our inherent happiness, we strive to rid ourselves of it. And from what we have experienced as a result of our direct observation, the only way to do this is to know with absolute certainty that the ego is not real. That is, it cannot be found. This awakening can be likened to letting go of a burning coal that we have been holding onto for eons.

Whenever the mind steadies and becomes quiet, we fix our attention on the emptiness, the stillness. With our old familiar habits of the mind and self-identifications behind us, we face the unknown and might wonder, *Am I this static void?* At this point, any perception or expectation we might have of the self must be abandoned along with the intellect. Just as a candle used to see things in the dark becomes useless in the presence of the sun, the intellect no longer serves a purpose. With full alertness and trust in the great unknown, we focus our attention on the one who becomes aware of awareness itself and realize it to be our true self.

The self is pure consciousness — the one and the same that is common to all beings. It is impersonal and often referred to as "the deathless" because it was never born nor will it ever die. Being formless, indiscernible to the physical senses, and equally present in the awake, dream and sleep states, the self has no limitations and is always accessible. It is our true teacher and the wellspring of grace. Hindu texts explain the self as a fusion of *being* or existence; *consciousness* or awareness; and *bliss* or happiness, peace and love. Beyond this, the self cannot be adequately explained in dualistic terms because, being the absolute, it transcends them. The self is not something found anew nor can it be attained, since we have never been apart from it for a single moment. If it were otherwise, the self would not be everlasting, permanent and true. And if it were something for us to gain, we would stand an equal chance of losing it. In truth, we have always been self-realized. Our pursuit is one of removing the ignorance that keeps us from knowing and, in turn, being the self.

Self-realization occurs when the mind has completely and permanently merged into the self. The illusion of "I" has been cast off, yet, paradoxically, "I" remains. "I" is perpetually being right here, right now, unlike a meditation period in which thoughts resume from where they left off once the meditation has ended. When a person is self-realized, the mental faculties continue to function as normal, yet without the interference of mind chatter, while interactions with others and daily routines are carried out as usual. In the presence of those who are self-realized, we might experience within ourselves a marked sense of clarity, happiness and peace. But aside from this, distinguishing characteristics common to all of them cannot be found.

While books and teachings on self-realization may kindle our interest, offer guidance and resolve some of our doubts, they only lead to more questions, since the nature of the mind is thought regeneration. Self-realization cannot be achieved by the intellect but rather through direct experience alone.

Our desire to be ever happy is proof of the unwavering happiness found in the self. We would not desire this if it were not already known to us. After all, we knew only happiness when we were born. Happiness is our very nature, not something that can be attained or defined by its opposite. Our desire to be ever happy is realized when we rid ourselves of the ignorance that keeps us from it. Thus, we let go of our thoughts and inquire, *Who am I?*.

When we realized that
we each perceived the world in different ways,
we let go of our perceptions and found each
other within our self.

To know the still mind
is all that need be known.

When the imaginary line between the inside, the seer,
and the outside, the seen,
ceases to exist, existence is realized to be eternal.

I am ever-present, eternal awareness,
nothing more and nothing less.
I am motionless and free of thoughts,
being ever peaceful and happy.
I am not a mind nor body within a world.
Instead, the mind, body and world emanate from me.
I am without words or concepts,
yet know all that need be known.
Knowing who I am is being who I am.
I am that I am.

The insatiable hunger of desire arising from the sense perceptions
is fed by the senseless fear of losing happiness – senseless,
in that it is our inherent nature and cannot be lost.

Look deep within the silence,
Well beyond the edges of the mind,
To where the formless light ever shines,
To where wordless clarity reveals reality,
To where boundless happiness has no opposite,
To where the question Who am I? is answered.

In this illusory world of individuality,
people strive to be the same
with the hope of being the best
when, in reality, everyone has always
been the best of the same.

To **accept** what is given and taken
To **comply** with what is requested
To **relinquish** what is unnecessary
without compromising ourselves
Is to **worship** the divinity
within us and all beings.

To see the manifestations of the body or the mind or the world
as anything other than an illusive play of the senses
is to lose sight of ourself.

Thoughts race in circles repeating
 endless stories of haunting themes.

Stories arouse fantasies and fears
 unleashing emotions as they go.

Emotions generate
 movement fueling the race
 with more thoughts.

Thoughts race in circles
 from one lifetime to the next,
 or until the thinker of them is held as reality no more.

Within the discernible gap
between thoughts
lies the ever-shining self
from which they arise and into
which they subside. All the while, the
ever shining is unaffected by any of them.

*O*ur desire to fill a sense of emptiness or incompleteness within ourselves or to gain acceptance or approval from others negates the very essence of our being. However, when this desire is turned inward by inquiring Who am I?, we realize that we have always been complete within ourselves.

The stream of thoughts
can become turbulent, like a raging river,
while its source is ever still and content within itself.

The phantom
within us, who pretends
to know all that need be known,
conceals the eternal one, who
knows all that is unknown.

No two human beings are exactly the same
in appearance, ability or behavior though
our true, underlying nature is exactly the same.
To love our true nature is to love all beings.

Life renews itself through endless repetitions of birth and death to a surreal design that flows in relation to, and as a result of, past actions. That is, until the cycle's existence is realized to be merely a dream-like projection emanating from the one reality — consciousness.

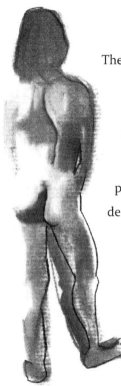

The primordial misconception of man —
I am the mind, body, senses
— is the root cause
of every form of human suffering.

This false assumption
pollutes the purity of awareness and
denies the omnipresence of happiness.

To hold fast to it
confines the boundless,
gives credence to delusion and
negates the eternal self.

To pause in the moment
and reflect upon it
is to realize that
it has neither
a beginning
nor an end —
the moment is eternal,
as is the one who realizes it.

I thought I knew
who I was.
However,
not until my mind
became completely still
did I begin to know
the truth of my existence
that I sensed I had always known
yet never knew.

When the thinker is sought rather than his thoughts followed,
his transparency is realized and his power is lost.
In his wake, the self alone remains.

To seek the thinker with relentless intent
brings about a steady abidance in the self, the one
who never leaves or changes and is forever happy.

*Imagined to be
an uncompromising
visitor, worry
demands our attention
while robbing the
inherent peace
of our being.*

W orries emerge from fear of the unknown
even though the unknown is the very source of peace.

Worries feed on the attention we give them.
If we ignore our worries, they lose their power and subside.

In the heart of the moment
Where the past and future do not exist
Where the body ceases to be mine
Where arising thoughts have nowhere to go
Where worldly pleasures have no command,
Is where I am.

In the heart of the moment
In which consciousness ever shines
In which existence never ends
In which happiness has no opposite
Is who I am.

Look not for an explicit answer
to the reflection **Who am I?**
but rather seek that which is changeless
and imperceptible to the senses — yet self-evident.

I wanted to be seen by the eyes of the world in some special way.

That is until I realized I was the eyes of the world.

For every thing lost
there is something gained, and
for every thing gained
there is something lost
in the world of duality.
However, in reality,
there is neither gain nor loss.

Concentration on things in motion engages the mind,
temporarily distracting it from its habitual thoughts.

Concentration on things that are steady calms the mind,
bringing lucidness and interim relief from its thoughts.

Concentration on the thinker of thoughts liberates the mind
obliterating the illusive thinker along with his thoughts.

Existence is self-evident
Being continuous without beginning or end
And distinct from the ever-changing mortal body.

Consciousness is self-evident
Being continuous without beginning or end
And distinct from the volatile thinking mind.

Bliss is self-evident
Being continuous without beginning or end
And distinct from the fleeting sensations of the senses.

Existence, consciousness and bliss are the self
Though they are indivisible from each other.
The self is continuous without beginning or end.

To seek happiness outside of ourselves
is forgetting that it lies within us.
Happiness is our very nature.

If your attempt
to follow the ways of the sage
brings discouragement that only distances
you from him, better to find the sage
in your heart, where he has always been,
and his ways will be yours as well.

In the throes of loss or despair
the blessings found in silence ever shine.

In the throes of anxiety or confusion,
the blessings found in silence ever shine.

In the throes of lust or aversion,
the blessings found in silence ever shine.

In the blessings of silence,
clarity, peace and joy ever reign.

Who clings to the finite when I am infinite?
Who claims to be the mind and body
when I am pure consciousness?
Who is captive to the demands of desire
when I am ever content and peaceful?
Who struggles to find himself
when I am always present?
Who is the imposter who poses to be who I am?

Only thoughts separate me from you, the negative ones as well as the positive.

Only thoughts separate me from myself, the negative ones as well as the positive.

The eternal light shines forth
from the one who relinquishes the known and familiar
for the sake of being that which is unknown and unfamiliar.

Driven by thoughts
into a world created by thoughts
and confined by endless cycles of thoughts —

Am I these choatic thoughts or am I the ever-peaceful
awareness that is detached from and untroubled by them?

Fascination

in something so familiar yet inexplicable,

so close yet untouchable,

so present yet invisible,

so peaceful yet vibrant,

so precious yet common,

so complete yet boundless,

so mystifying yet illuminating.

Fascination

in the silence of an introverted mind.

The purpose of life
is to master the
art of surrender,

which ultimately includes
the I-am-the-mind-body perception.

A _quiescent yet vibrant_ mind
in which the incessant flow of
extraneous thoughts have been
quelled by vigilant persistence that requires
utmost patience and humility is, indeed, one to behold.

The one
who judges,
criticizes
or blames others

is the same one who finds fault in himself. Consequently,
he alienates not only others but himself as well. To find the
blameless one within oneself is to find the same in all beings.

Essential knowledge,
common to all, is found in the source of
thoughts, where nothing is as it is thought
to be, yet everything is as it is intended.

The solitary journey of
self-realization
is not a journey at all,
since the self has never
been apart.
Nor could it be solitary,
since nothing exists
outside of the self.

From the eternal self, which is unalloyed consciousness,
   all is seen as a fleeting illusion.

From the imagined self, which is part of the illusion,
   all is seen as real.

The fleeting illusion is not apart from the eternal self.

The love that
has no beginning
or end is experienced
when the assumed
perceptions we have of
ourselves are abandoned.

When the chain of thoughts
of unimaginable strength,
which is composed solely of
fleeting desires, memories and perceptions
that are dearly yet fearfully held onto and
collectively define the isolating notion of individuality,
is

a luminosity of
irrepressible magnitude, vibrancy and grandeur
is experienced as
the lightness of being.

In pursuit of self knowledge

the inquiring mind looks not into the ever-changing world questioning Why? or How? but rather inward onto itself questioning Who? and From where?

Undivided attention placed on
The thinker rather than his thoughts
The worrier rather than his worries
The fearful one rather than his fears
The craver rather than his cravings
Enables the dreamer to awaken.

Time moves in accordance with thoughts. Without them, there is neither time nor the interplay of the objective world that occurs within time. What remains in the absence of thoughts is timeless — omnipresent, immutable and ever peaceful.

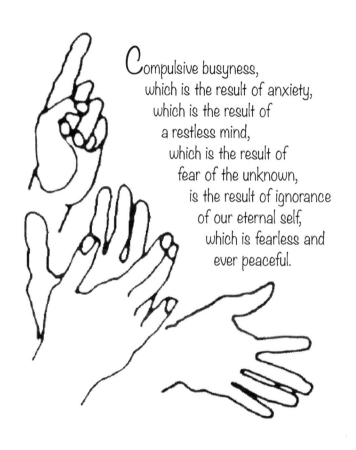

Compulsive busyness,
which is the result of anxiety,
which is the result of
a restless mind,
which is the result of
fear of the unknown,
is the result of ignorance
of our eternal self,
which is fearless and
ever peaceful.

What is true for the boy
is not true for him when he becomes a man.

What is true for the dreamer
is not true for him when he awakens.

Only the one who prevails throughout the changing states is true.

Who is the one who chooses to believe in mere concepts about
the unknown when it is far more telling
to simply believe in the unknown?

We create our own suffering

by resenting the
challenges that
come our way or
imagining we can
control them. All the
while, we fail to inquire
Who is suffering?

If we had, the sufferer would not be found to be ever
present and suffering would lose its underlying basis.

Suffering is the means of liberating habits of the mind.
It comes and goes. Yet, all the while, happiness always is.

The phenomenal world serves as a reflection of my existence. Like a dream, it is an illusory projection of myself upon myself.

Though the world is ever changing, I am not.

Though the world expresses itself in opposites, I do not.

And though the world is not apart from me, its very appearance confirms my existence as the formless and inconceivable substratum upon which it appears.

Memories of the past and dreams of the future
base their existence on thoughts, which are subject
to change and, accordingly, have no lasting reality.
What is real never changes.

The timeless love, which always was
and still is, will forever be.

The world is only imperfect
to our perception of perfection.

Are there two subjects, namely the subject that sees only the object and another that sees both the subject and the object?

Could there be two of me?

Surely the one who sees the other must be who I am.

The eternal moment holds neither a past nor a future. For this reason, it is devoid of conditioned likes and dislikes or doubts and fears. It is from which all actions originate. Though neither words nor concepts can be found within it, the eternal moment is the source of indisputable knowledge and the pinnacle of joyfulness. The eternal moment is always accessible, indivisible and complete within itself.

Could we ever be anywhere other than in the eternal moment? If so, who is that one?

*W*ith steady abidance in the unwavering, eternal self
from which the seer is seen along with the seen,
our daily work is completed,
interactions with others are harmonious,
and happiness is uninterrupted.

Life changes come
as they may —
sometimes fulfilling
dreams and other times
destroying them.

Yet all life changes bring blessings of equal measure.

Wisdom is that
which is always known
but often forgotten or ignored.

Spiritual traditions that idealize perfection fail to consider that man is already perfect — veiled only by the erroneous perception he has of himself. To realize perfection nothing new need be gained, only the false sense of self must be dispelled by inquirying Who am I?.

The mother brings life to the baby
while she is but the witness.

The sun brings life to the earth
while it is but the witness,

Consciousness brings life to the cosmos,
while it is but the witness.

*The mind becomes active to acquire things,
fulfill desires, resolve problems, confirm beliefs.
But when the mind is still,
as in dreamless sleep,
there are no things, desires, problems or beliefs.*

The mind is not capable of perceiving
what pure consciousness holds to be true.

What is external to the self is terminal.

What is internal to the self is eternal.

What is external is not apart from the internal.

To guide others
does not mean to control their ways,
but rather to love them as ourself.

The search for our truth is not a search at all.

Instead, it is the act of letting go of the perceptions
we hold to be true.

In its entirety,
diversity is singular
presenting unity as perfection.
But if diversity provokes separation,
it becomes divisive and unity is lost.

The self can neither be found in the mind
nor understood through the mind's thoughts.

The self can neither be found in the body
nor understood through the body's senses.

The self can neither be found,
since it cannot be lost, nor understood,
since its knowledge cannot be surpassed.

To know the self is to be the self.
To be the self is to know the self.

To vigilantly stalk
the illusory self—the one who is governed by
restlessness, torpor and fear — is to kill it.

Floundering between
past confusions and future uncertainties?

Be right here, right now

and the rest will take care of itself.

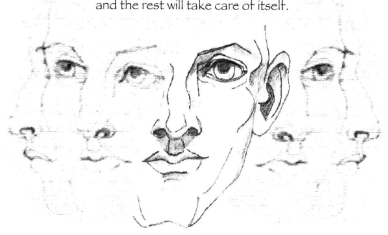

The dualistic view of the active mind knows
reality as oppositions —
To know light, there must be darkness
To know love, there must be hatred
To know peace, there must be conflict
To know happiness, there must be suffering
The monistic view of the still mind knows
reality as only light, love, peace and happiness.

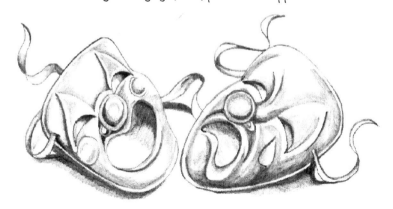

The intellect cannot comprehend the essential
knowledge that is accessible to
the still mind alone.

When thoughts are believed to be oneself,
the space between them appears to be empty.
However, when that space is focused upon,
thoughts are seen to be empty and
the space is realized to be the eternal self.

Can the act of doing be completed without the one who claims doership?

The one who appears only randomly, if at all, during the act,
who demands its expectations be fulfilled,
who clamors for recognition, and
whose mere presence hinders concentration?
If that one is not ever present, the question is answered.

Evidence
based on sight is taken as
the seal of truth though it
fails to take into
account that
sight,
the act of seeing
and the seer
all derive from
the same singular consciousness that alone holds the truth.

From outward mind to inward mind,
discerning the real, which is enduring,
from the unreal, which is fleeting,
is the practice, which is not a practice at all.
It is simply being true to ourselves.

What lies beyond the universe
is not found outside of ourselves but within.

Until the seeker realizes that he alone is the one being sought, questions will continue to arise.

Though I perceive the world through the senses of a particular body, I am no more this body than any other body. In truth, I am as much outside this body as I am inside of it and experience neither distinction nor separation from anything. I have full awareness and knowledge of all that comes and goes, yet I am impervious to any of it.

Amid the ever-changing phenomena, an unexplainable phantom appeared who, upon having first seen this particular body, claimed it to be himself. Then, he took full credit and blame for all of its activities. But this phantom has no control over any of them. Instead, the activities are solely manifestations of his own past actions and repeat themselves as tendencies, or habits of the mind, over and over again, throughout the duration of this particular body. And when this body perishes, he quickly claims another to perpetuate his tendencies.

This illusive sense of self has no substance whatsoever— he is simply a figment that has mysteriously materialized due to the false notion that the world is outside of himself and becomes enlived by the sensations of the senses with their ephemeral pleasures. Imprisoned from one lifetime to the next in this spurious notion, the imagined self struggles to gain happiness and peace of being. And all the while, I, the eternal self, have never been without them.